JEZ BUTTERWORTH

Mojo (1995), *The Night Heron* (2002), *The Winterling* (2006), *Jerusalem* (2009) and *The River* (2012) were all premiered at the Royal Court Theatre, London. *Jerusalem* transferred to the Apollo Theatre in London's West End in 2010, the Music Box Theatre, New York, in 2011, and back to the Apollo later in 2011. *Parlour Song* was premiered at the Atlantic Theater, New York, in 2008, and at the Almeida Theatre, London, in 2009. *Mojo* won the George Devine Award, the Olivier Award for Best Comedy and the Writers' Guild, Critics' Circle and Evening Standard Awards for Most Promising Playwright. *Jerusalem* won the Best Play Award at the Critics' Circle, Evening Standard and WhatsOnStage.com Awards, and was nominated for the Tony Award for Best Play. Jez wrote and directed the film adaptation of *Mojo* (1998) starring Ian Hart and Harold Pinter, and *Birthday Girl* (2002) starring Nicole Kidman and Ben Chaplin, and co-wrote and produced *Fair Game* (2010) starring Sean Penn and Naomi Watts. In 2007 he was awarded the E.M. Forster Award by the American Academy of Arts and Letters.

Jez Butterworth

THE WINTERLING

NICK HERN BOOKS

London

www.nickhernbooks.co.uk

A Nick Hern Book

The Winterling first published in Great Britain as a paperback original in 2006 by Nick Hern Books Limited, The Glasshouse, 49a Goldhawk Road, London W12 8QP, in association with the Royal Court Theatre, London

Reprinted in this revised edition 2008, 2010, 2011, 2012

The Winterling copyright © 2006, 2008 Jez Butterworth

Jez Butterworth has asserted his right to be identified as the author of this work

Cover image: Lisa Johansson

Typeset by Country Setting, Kingsdown, Kent CT14 8ES
Printed in Great Britain by Mimeo Ltd, Huntingdon, Cambridgeshire PE29 6XX

A CIP catalogue record for this book is available from the British Library

ISBN   978 1 85459 926 1

For Shena Malone

The Winterling was first performed at the Royal Court Theatre
Downstairs, London, on 2 March 2006, with the following cast:

DRAYCOTT   Roger Lloyd Pack
LUE   Sally Hawkins
PATSY   Daniel Mays
WALLY   Jerome Flynn
WEST   Robert Glenister

Director   Ian Rickson
Designer   Ultz
Lighting Designer   Johanna Town
Sound Designer   Ian Dickinson
Music   Stephen Warbeck

The dog starv'd at its Master's gate
Predicts the ruin of the State.

William Blake

Characters

in order of appearance

WEST, *forties*

DRAYCOTT, *forties*

WALLY, *forties*

PATSY, *twenty-five*

LUE, *twentyish*

The action takes place in an abandoned farmhouse in the centre of the forest of Dartmoor.

Act One begins in the dead of winter. Act Two begins in the previous winter. Act Three is the first winter again.

ACT ONE

Darkness. Distant shelling. Small arms fire. Closer. All at once, overhead, the deafening cacophony of war. Just when it can't get any louder it fades into

Light.

Dartmoor. The heart of the frozen forest, on clenched, sideways land. Sheep. Far off, a dog barking.

A deserted, half-derelict farmhouse. Doors off. Stairs up.

A rat-gnawed armchair. Small table, with no chairs. A large axe waits by a giant inglenook fireplace. The fireback is a red-rusty circular saw. Dark windows look onto an area beyond; a concrete floor utility room, in which stands a mangle, a piece of red canvas protruding from its jaws like a lapping tongue.

From an overhead drier hangs a black woollen suit, waiting.

Suddenly, warplanes burst over, looming, shuddering. The full blaring cacophony of... It passes, back to a rumble in the distance.

Blackout.

Lights.

WEST *stands wearing the woollen suit.*

A brace of duck hangs in the kitchen, where the suit was.

WEST *takes a bottle of wine and pulls the cork. He places it on the table, with three glasses.*

WEST. Dolly. Din Dins. Dolly. Din Dins. (*He goes to the cupboard. Opens a tin of dog food.*) Din Dins, Dolly. Dolly! DOLLY!! DIN DINS.

Puts it in a bowl, carries it to the door.

DOLLY. DIN DINS. DIN DINS. DIN DINS.

Nothing. He cocks his head. The planes approach. As they scream over, he opens his mouth wide, as if to…

Blackout.

Lights.

WEST. *Opposite him,* DRAYCOTT.

DRAYCOTT. Sorry to bother you. (*Pause.*) I was just passing. I heard a din. A man it was. Top of his lungs. Yelling his bonce off. Did you hear it?

WEST. The dog's gone off. (*Pause.*)

DRAYCOTT. The little fella. I seen him. Oftentimes, I'm up this way, early morn. He's gone off, you say?

WEST. She.

DRAYCOTT. I see. Bitch, is it? You had her done? You've got to watch 'em, bitches. If she's ripe. Out there looking for it, no doubt. You want to watch that one. She'll come home got.

WEST. What do you want?

DRAYCOTT. I was on my way over Okement Foot. They're gassing the badgers. It was on the radio. There's a mighty sett down Okement Foot. Been taking hens. Pheasants. All the way from here to Dolton. They got coughs too. Hacking coughs. The government's had enough. They're sending a team in. Experts. What do you say? Eh? You want in? He's not far. Three, four mile, across the fields. He's a mighty sett. An underground city. Might be worth it. Might be something. Can I tempt you? What do you say?

WEST. I'm busy. (*Pause.*)

DRAYCOTT. Oh. Well, that's that. If you're busy. Say no more. If a man's busy… (*Beat.*) I had a fight with a badger once. Wphew! It's a long story. Don't go there. Lost three pints of blood to it. And a nipple. By the way, you haven't got any Dettol, have you?

WEST. What?

DRAYCOTT. I fell yesterday. In the dark. I've chipped my hip. He's tightening. The skin's broke. There's a flap of sorts. I was thinking of staunching the pain. Dettol's my best bet. Itches. Stitches, palsies or gout, Dettol's the boy. You wouldn't keep a supply, would you? Any linament? Oinment, what have you...?

WEST. No.

DRAYCOTT. Sprays? Unguents?

WEST. I've got no ointments. I've got no sprays. I can't help you.

DRAYCOTT. No harm asking. I'll just have to keep him mobile.

WEST. Why don't you do that?

DRAYCOTT. Exactly. I will.

WEST. Better not stop too long. He might seize up.

DRAYCOTT. You're not wrong.

WEST. Get infected. Gangrenous. Then where would you be?

DRAYCOTT. Don't. They'll lop me to pieces. Butchers they are, with the likes of me. Before I know it I'll be in three bin bags and down the chute. By the way, is it still convenient?

WEST. Is what convenient?

DRAYCOTT. The arrangement.

WEST. What arrangement?

DRAYCOTT. Have I got this wrong? About... about the porch. I don't want to be a pain. I won't make a mess or a smell. I'll be gone at first light. Like I was never there.

WEST. Yes.

DRAYCOTT. That's awful kind. There won't be a trace. Above all, there won't be no mess nor smell. You'll never even know I was –

WEST. No. I mean Yes. Yes I do mind.

Pause.

DRAYCOTT. Oh.

WEST. It's not convenient. It's not convenient at all.

DRAYCOTT. Oh dear. I've got this wrong.

WEST. Come back tomorrow.

DRAYCOTT. I see. You're busy. Say no more. You're expecting someone. Is that a drop of brandy wine I see? I bet he's a vintage. Is he a nice drop? French, is he?

WEST. It's none of your business. (*Beat.*) Just stay back for one day. You come back tomorrow, I'll have something for you.

DRAYCOTT (*of the brace of duck*). I noticed them. They're beauties, they are. Full in the breast. Say no more. I'll stay back. You won't hear a peep. In fact, I'll start right now.

WEST. Why don't you do that?

DRAYCOTT. It's a juicy piece that. I know a recipe. I'm a good cook, me. I've cooked all over. I once cooked for fifty-six turf accountants. (*Beat.*) Well that's that. I'm off. And if I see that bitch of yours, I'll send her up the track. It's Okement Foot, if you change your mind. Those badgers don't know what they got coming. All warm in their holes. Bedding down. They don't know what's next.

Pause. He leaves. WEST *looks at his watch. He picks up the dog bowl.*

WEST. Dolly. Din Dins. Din Dins.

A plane screams over. He goes out the side door.

After some time, from the door out at the back, through the utility room, enter WALLY *in suit and winter coat. He is soaking, caked in mud from the knee down. He looks around. He looks at the wine.*

Enter PATSY, *in leather jacket. He is also caked in mud from the knee down. While* PATSY *speaks,* WALLY *regards the three chairs. The wine glasses. He goes over. Pours himself a glass. Sniffs it. Looks at it…*

PATSY. Just for the record, did I say, 'Don't rev it. (*Beat*.)
    Wally, don't spin the wheels. Just let her off, slowly. Let it
    bite.' (*Beat*.) Or. Did I say, 'Whatever you do, Wally, fuckin'
    floor it. Do a donut. In this boggy, soggy field. Dig me,
    Wally, a lovely big hole. Halfway to China.' (*Beat*.) That
    car's finished, mate. It's a landmark. In fifty thousand years,
    they will come in their hordes, gaze upon it and say, 'That
    was Wally done that. He must have revved it.' (*Beat*.) Don't
    worry. I found my way up here. Half a mile. No torch. Could
    have sworn I brung one. Oh, there is it. In your hand. It's not
    like it's pitch black out there. It's not like I completely lost the
    path after fifty yards, ended up bumbling through brambles.
    Fucking stingers up to here. It's not like I had to swim a con-
    siderable part of the way. Quick question Wally. Do you
    know who Ozwald Boateng is?

WALLY (*sips the wine. Pause*). This coffee is cold.

PATSY. I'm not talking to you.

WALLY. This coffee is cold. (*Beat*.) This muffin is stale.

PATSY. I said. I'm not talk –

WALLY. This muffin's stale. It's dry.

PATSY. Did you taste it? It was like rock. Like a rock someone
    sprayed brown. What do you want me to say? 'Ooh this is
    lovely, Wally. Thank you for this poo muffin. Thank you for
    this shit service-station coffee and rock-hard muffin. Thank
    you for this delightful… ' Did you bake it, mate? Did you
    bake that muffin?

WALLY. The car's too hot.

PATSY. How much was it? Ninety pence? Go on. Just for a bit
    of peace and quiet.

WALLY. It's too hot. My heated seat is stuck on hot.

PATSY. Is it your car? No. It's not. Try the passenger seat, mate.
    It's like a fucking Turkish bath. I lost about a stone on the
    M4 alone.

WALLY. What *do* you like, Patsy?

PATSY. I like London, Wally. I like pavements. I like to walk out the door and not sink up to my tits in primordial sludge. I don't like sheep. I don't like Dartmoor. I don't like the country. It's covered in shit.

Pause.

WALLY. You uptight, Patsy?

PATSY. Not me.

WALLY. You seem nervous.

PATSY. Why would I be nervous?

WALLY. You're not going to have one of your nosebleeds, are you? Make me look silly?

PATSY. I'm not nervous.

WALLY. You seem it.

PATSY. Well I'm not.

WALLY (*without moving*). Hello Mr West.

The light changes, behind in the utility room, revealing WEST from the shadows. Only then, he moves forward.

WEST. Hello Wally. (*Pause.*)

WALLY. The door was open. There was a light on. (*Pause.*)

WEST. The dog's run off.

WALLY. Has he?

WEST. She.

WALLY. Bitch, is it?

WEST. Muddy, was it?

WALLY. We lost the path.

WEST. You do what I say? Turn left at the hill.

WALLY. Thing is, yes. Thing is… There's loads of hills.

WEST. You turn right at the sheep.

WALLY. We did. We did. Thing is –

WEST. Turn left at the hill, right at the sheep, you can't go wrong. You want to watch that track up. It's treacherous. Each spring, when the snow clears, they find three or four down there. It's ramblers mostly. Last ones they brung up was a couple of Welsh. Just married too. Skeletons they was. Huddled together. He'd been Young Welsh Businessman of the Year. What took you so long?

WALLY. The rivers are up. We got to Bridgetown, the road was closed.

WEST. Bridgetown.

WALLY. The Bridgetown road was closed. Something to do with the bridge.

WEST. The bridge at Bridgetown.

WALLY. It's been condemned.

WEST. The bridge at Bridgetown's been condemned? Well. That's bad news for Bridgetown. That's a disaster for Bridgetown, you'd have to say.

WALLY. We had to go the long way round. The car got stuck. It's only a little two-seater.

WEST. A two-seater.

WALLY. We come up on foot from the road.

WEST. You see the fort.

WALLY. The what?

WEST. You pass by the fort? Iron Age fort. You can't miss it. Been there since the Iron Age.

WALLY. That's just it. It was that dark –

WEST. But you can't have missed it. You go straight through it. You must've blundered clean through it. Now you're all muddy, you must be perishing. You want to pop yourself in front of the fire. Don't stand on ceremony. Come in. Come in. Make yourself at home. I see you found the wine.

WALLY. Yes.

WEST. Is she a nice drop?

WALLY. It is. It's very tasty.

WEST. He was always fond of a red. That was his tipple. Red. So bloody hell, Wally.

WALLY. I know.

WEST. Bloody hell.

WALLY. Bloody hell.

WEST. Don't. Please.

WALLY. Three. Four years.

WEST. And the rest.

WALLY. Must be. Must be.

WEST. How've you been, son?

WALLY. Mustn't grumble.

WEST. Don't give me that.

WALLY. I toddle along.

WEST. Don't give me that. You're a picture of it. The very picture.

WALLY. Nothing changes.

WEST. Bollocks, mate. You look ten years younger.

WALLY. Time flies.

WEST. Fuller, but younger. You're a breath of fresh air.

WALLY. Am I? Fuller though…

WEST. Bollocks. You're a fresh breeze and no mistake. That hair lacquer? You been at the boot polish?

WALLY. Not me, Mr West.

WEST. You lacquering the mane. That Just for Men?

WALLY. Just for Ladies more like. From here down…

WEST. You dirty git. That's my Wally. That's my Wally. Seriously, chum, you been at the cold cream. Got a stylist now, have you? They had you in a tank? Up there in the smoke. You're all at it. I bet you've got a dermatologist, you gay prat.

WALLY. Cheeky sod!

WEST. That's more like it. So what is it then? Up there in the smoke. All the latest. You've had a face-peel. Admit it. You've been under the knife, you gay berk.

WALLY. You look well yourself.

WEST. Fresh air, Wally. No hokey-pokey. Hundred press-ups for breakfast. Squat thrusts for lunch. Star jumps for prayers. Pelting across fields. Come rain or snow. Not tucked up in some fucking clinic. Rigged up to some poncey piece of kit. Paying through the nose like a fucking woman. Look at you. Look at yourself. Look at yourself. I've missed you, Wally.

WALLY. I've missed you too, Len. Come here.

WEST. Where's Jerry?

Silence.

WALLY. He's not here.

WEST. I can see he's not here. Where is he?

WALLY. He couldn't make it.

WEST. Couldn't make it?

WALLY. Thing is… see. He couldn't come.

WEST. He couldn't come.

WALLY. No. So I brung Patsy.

Pause.

WEST. Who's Patsy? Who's Patsy, Wally?

WALLY. This is Patsy. Patsy, Mr West. Len, Patsy. (*Beat.*)

WEST. Watcha, Patsy.

PATSY. Watcha, Mr West.

WEST. Who's Patsy?

PATSY. He's –

WEST. Patsy.

PATSY. Yes.

WEST. Who's Patsy, Wally? Who's Patsy?

WALLY. This is Patsy.

WEST. Is this him? Is this Patsy?

WALLY. Yes.

WEST. You're all dirty, Patsy. You're covered. You're worse
    than Wally.

PATSY. I'm a bit mucky.

WEST. You're a state, Patsy. You're filthy. We'll need to give
    you a bath. You cold, Patsy? You want to stand by the fire?

PATSY. Actually –

WEST. We spoke, Wally. We spoke on the phone.

WALLY. We did. We did.

WEST. You remember?

WALLY. You was in some phone box.

WEST. I tried to call Jerry. I couldn't get Jerry. So I called
    Wally. And what did I say?

WALLY. You said –

WEST. What did I say, Wally?

WALLY. You said –

WEST. I said bring Jerry.

WALLY. Len –

WEST. Jerry, Wally.

WALLY. Len –

WEST. Jerry, Wally –

WALLY. Len –

WEST. It's not pick-your-own strawberries, Wally. Come one, come all. Where's Jerry? I asked for Jerry.

WALLY. Len –

WEST. Where's Jerry, Wally? I asked for Jerry. Where's Jerry, Wally? Where's Jerry?

WALLY. Jerry's dead. (*Pause*.) He died. (*Pause*.) He's no longer with us. He passed on last March.

WEST. How? (*Beat*.)

WALLY. He jumped in the Thames.

Pause.

WEST. He jumped in the Thames.

WALLY. Yes, Mr West. He jumped in the Thames.

Silence.

WEST. Why don't you stand in front of the fire, Patsy? Like Wally. Warm yourself. You're all mucky. That's it. (*Beat*.) It's nice and warm. Isn't it?

WALLY. It's toasty.

WEST. See? Get in there, snug next door.

PATSY. Thanks, Mr West.

WEST. That's better. Dry yourself off. You pair of twerps. That's better. Forgive me. I'm catching up. Patsy is –

WALLY. Right. Patsy's my…

WEST. Yes.

PATSY. I'm his –

WALLY. He's my stepson.

WEST. Are you his stepson? Are you his boy?

PATSY. Yes. (*Beat*.) Well no. Well yes. Sort of.

WEST. Are you or aren't you?

PATSY. Well –

WEST. Forgive me, Wally. I'm just catching up.

WALLY. See, the thing is Len…

PATSY. What Wally is –

WALLY (*interrupting*). Stay out of this, Patsy –

PATSY. What?

WALLY. What I'm trying to say is –

PATSY (*interrupting*). Wally's with my mum. He's seeing my mum. He's… you know… (*Beat.*) With my mum.

WEST. What you talking about? Wally's with Sarah.

WALLY. Well that's just it.

WEST. You're with Sarah. Lovely Sarah.

WALLY. See, that's just it, Len.

WEST. It was Wally and Sarah. Wally and Sarah.

PATSY. Not any more. Sarah left him.

WEST. Is this true, Wally? Has Patsy got this right?

WALLY. You know how it is, Len. Matters of the heart. Situations change. People drift apart. It was six of one –

PATSY. She was shagging some Turk.

WALLY. Half a dozen the other –

PATSY. She run off with some Turk. To Turkey.

WALLY. Shut it.

PATSY. Now it's Rita.

WEST. Who's Rita?

PATSY. My mum.

WEST. Since when?

WALLY. Two years March.

WEST. Why didn't you say? You're with his mum. Here I am. Eh? Here I am… He's your boy. This is your boy.

WALLY. Well –

WEST. You're his boy…

PATSY. Well see…

WEST. Why didn't somebody tell me. You'll have to forgive me. I'm catching up. Father and son. Man and boy.

WALLY. Sort of. Exactly.

PATSY. Yes and no. Not really but yes. Exactly.

WEST. Me and your old man, Patsy. Me and the old man. We go back. Has he told you? I bet he did. I bet he did. He told you, didn't he? What did he tell you? What did he tell you, Patsy? What did he tell you? Did he leave out the best bits? The dirty stuff. You don't know the half of it. I'll tell you stories'll put hair on your chest. You got hair on your chest, Patsy?

PATSY. I have as it happens.

WEST. I bet you have. So that's that. You're a hairy boy. Bloody hell, Wally. They grow up fast, don't they?

WALLY. Well see, I've only known Patsy for –

WEST. You turn your back for five minutes. It's horrifying. Hang on. You uncomfortable, Patsy? You uncomfortable in your soggy trousers?

PATSY. It's not as bad as it looks, Mr West.

WEST *walks forward, stands in front of* PATSY.

WEST. May I?

PATSY. What?

He kneels, maintaining eye contact. Slowly, he feels the bottom of the trouser.

WEST. Whoops-a-daisy. (*He stands.*) Someone's telling whoppers. Patsy's sopping, Wally. He's soaked to the bone.

PATSY. I'm fine actually.

WEST. Nonsense, Wally. You know what he should do? You know what you should do, Patsy? You should pop them off. Hang them in front of the fire. They'll dry in no time. Go on, Patsy. Pop your slacks off. Pop them off. (*Pause*.) Why don't you pop yours off, Wally? Show him how it's done. Pop them off, Wally. (*Pause*.)

WALLY. They are quite muddy.

WEST. Muddy? They're caked. Come on, you prat. We'll have them dry in no time. Take your slacks off, Wally. Show him how it's done.

WALLY. Well then. That's that, isn't it?

Beat. WALLY *takes his trousers off.*

WEST. That's the way. Off they come. That's it.

WALLY *stands there, holding them.*

Now just like Dad, Patsy. Just like the old man. Follow the old man.

WALLY. Come on. Mr West is right.

WEST. There's no point stood there. We're halfway there.

PATSY *undoes his belt. He takes them off.*

That's the way. That's the way.

PATSY *tosses them to* WEST *who catches them. Pause.*

And the funny thing is, I wouldn't say you were that hairy after all. I'd say you were average. Nothing to write home about.

PATSY. Thanks, Mr West. I appreciate that.

WEST. So what do you think, Dad? Can he have a glass of wine?

WALLY. What? Oh. Yes. Of course. Sure.

WEST. Is that all right? I don't want to, you know.

WALLY. No. He likes wine. I think.

WEST. Patsy?

WALLY. Yes he does. Of course he does. He loves a drop.
Don't you, Patsy?

WEST. You take after Dad, Patsy. Drop of the old red. You
fancy a drop. Like the old man?

PATSY. If it's all the same, Mr West, I'll have a Scotch.

Pause.

WEST. You sure? You sure, Patsy?

PATSY. If it's all the same.

Pause.

WEST. Well that's that, isn't it? Wally's red. Patsy's a Scotch.
Hang about, Patsy. I'll fetch you one. Don't you worry. I'll
warm you up.

He takes WALLY's, *and hangs up the trousers.*

So you came, Wally. You came.

WALLY. Yes we did. We did, sir. We did.

Silence. Exit WEST. *They stand there, side by side, trouser-
less, before the fire. A plane tears over. They both duck.
Silence.*

PATSY. Nice man. What?

WALLY. 'I'll have a Scotch.'

PATSY. He's asked me a question. You said. You said in the car.
If he asks you a question –

WALLY. Soda? Cherry? On the rocks?

PATSY. You said. Look him in the eye –

WALLY. Umbrella? Angostura bitters?

PATSY. – tell the truth. You said. Tell the truth. Well the truth is
I fancied a Scotch.

WALLY. I've got a hairy chest.

PATSY. I can't drink wine, Wally. It gives me the hives. I go
blotchy. What do you want me to do? Drink it down, have a
fit on the man's carpet. How's that going to help?

WALLY. You tit.

PATSY. Wally –

WALLY. You prannock. You prannie. Keep your big mouth shut.

PATSY. It's just a Scotch.

WALLY. Keep your big gob shut.

PATSY. OK. I'm sorry.

WALLY. You blundering tit.

PATSY. I said I'm sorry. I'm sorry. *(Beat.)* Daddy.

Beat. WALLY *glares.*

Well we sorted that out.

WALLY. What?

PATSY. I think he seems fine. I don't think he seems (PATSY
makes the mad sign with his finger to his head.) at all.
I mean, look at it. There's three of us here. Right now, he's
the only one still got his trousers on. So go on.

WALLY. What?

PATSY. I don't want to rush you. It's just this seems a good
time to ask.

WALLY. What? Ask what?

PATSY. The phone rings. 'Patsy. Ten o'clock. Outside
Costcutters.' Passport. Toothbrush. Roll-on. Bam. I'm
there. No questions asked.

WALLY. Patsy –

PATSY. M4. M5. Not a sausage. Not a squeak. Not a prob.
Wally's in charge. The all-giving, all-seeing Wally. But now
we're here, now we have this moment alone, in our pants... I
don't need the blueprints. I don't need a slideshow. Just

throw me a bone, Wally. What's going on? I mean, where do you want me, skipper?

WALLY. Shut your cakehole, leave this to me.

PATSY. See, that's just it, Wally. I was leaving it to you. And now I'm stood here in my pants. We both are. You look nervous, Wally. You're sweating. You are. Your top lip is shiny.

WALLY. Here we go.

PATSY. Your armpits are pouring. You've kicked right up. The glands have gone.

WALLY. Here we fucking go.

PATSY. You've done your trick. Your nervous trick. Like that barbecue. 'Oh my marinade's too salty.' You've gone up chum. You've done the Sweaty Wally.

WALLY. Fuck off.

PATSY. You have. I can smell you. Dead of winter and you're sweating like a rapist. (*Offering him a roll-on.*) You want to roll on, chum? I don't mind.

WALLY. Why don't you have a nosebleed?

PATSY. I'm not having a nosebleed, am I? But you're indisputably doing the Sweaty Wally. Anyone can see it. Mr West can see it. He can smell it. Take the roll-on, Wally. Don't be proud.

WALLY. You want to go back to washing cars. Eh? Rolling cabbies on the Great West Way? Don't bite the hand, Patsy. You're lucky to be here. There's five or six blokes –

PATSY. Here we go.

WALLY. Fuck off. There's six or seven blokes could be stood here in your shoes.

PATSY. I bet they're right jealous. Six hours in a car with Wally. Shit coffee. Poo muffin. I bet they're all crying into their pillows. Verily. For I am the chosen one.

WALLY. You watch your step –

PATSY. So what is my task, O Wally? Fight a Centaur? Steal
Mr West's magic bow? What is the task I am so honoured to
perform by you, O Wally? O Sweaty Wally?

WALLY. You keep it down, you bumboy. Watch your step, you
squashy-headed nit. I'm watching you, bumboy. Don't bite
the hand.

PATSY. Why are you sweating? Eh? Wally? What's he doing
here? In the middle of nowhere. Throw me a bone, Wally.
Throw me a bone.

WALLY. You want to wake up tomorrow? Get back in that car?
Eh? You want to spend the rest of your life in some home
doing jigsaws. Colouring things in. Wake up spread all over
some field. I'll throw you a bone, Patsy. You don't know
where you are. You Don't Know Where You Are.

PATSY. Please, Daddy. You're scaring us.

WALLY. Watch your step. Watch your step, son.

PATSY. You watch your step, son. (*Pause.*)

Re-enter WEST.

WEST. Patsy, you're in luck. By chance. I keep half a bottle
upstairs. Under the sink. I rub it on my tummy when I've
got the flu.

PATSY. I'm sorry to be so much trouble, Mr West.

WEST. Don't be gay, Patsy. It's a pleasure. Now I warn you. It's
not a malt. It's not some prim job's sat in a barrel since the
First World War. It's not been filtered through six millennia of
granite and peat nor sieved through Rob Roy's sporran. It's
good old-fashioned, straight up and down Tesco's Scottish
Whisky. I like it that way. Let's see if you like it that way too.

PATSY. Let's.

He pours. Raises it.

WEST. A toast. To the newcomers. (*Pause.*)

WALLY. To the newcomers.

WEST *regards* PATSY, *who knocks it back.*

PATSY. You know what that is, Mr West? That is extremely palatable. It don't taste cheap and nasty at all. (*Beat.*)

WEST. So who's your mum?

WALLY. What?

PATSY. What?

WALLY. Rita.

WEST. Rita?

WALLY. You know Rita.

WEST. No I don't.

WALLY. Yes you do. Rita.

WEST. Who's Rita? (*Stops.*) Rita?

WALLY. Yes.

WEST. That Rita?

WALLY. Yeah.

WEST. I see. (*Beat.*)

WALLY. Yes, Len.

WEST. You're with Rita.

WALLY. Yes, Len. Patsy's mum.

Pause. WEST *doesn't take his eyes off* PATSY.

Bugger.

WEST. What?

WALLY. Blast.

WEST. What's wrong, Wally? What is it?

WALLY. I've left my fags in the car.

WEST. Oh no.

WALLY. I only have.

WEST. You nit.

WALLY. I'm always doing that.

WEST. You berk.

WALLY. They're in the blessed glove compartment.

WEST. Wally…

WALLY. I am. I'm that big a tonk. (*Beat.*) I tell you what. You want to fetch them, Patsy?

PATSY. What?

WALLY. You want to fetch my fags? My Lamberts. I've left them in the motor. In the blessed glove compartment.

PATSY. You want a Benson? I got heaps.

WEST. Nothing doing. If I know Wally.

WALLY. I smoke Lamberts. Always have.

WEST. Always has. If I know Wally.

WALLY. Been smoking Lamberts for thirty years.

WEST. You could say he's a Lamberts man.

WALLY. They're in the glove compartment, Patsy. Failing that, there's a duty-free carton in the boot. In my bowling bag. Tucked inside my bowling bag. You want to fetch me a packet?

PATSY. It's half a mile.

WALLY. It's downhill.

PATSY. It's pitch dark.

WALLY. Take the torch. Please, Patsy. I would like it. Please, son. Fetch my fags. Fetch my fags. Fetch them. Fetch.

Pause. PATSY *fetches his trousers.*

WEST. A word of advice, Patsy. The path. It's deceptively slippy on the way back down. Off to the left is a sheer drop. It falls away to nothing. My tip: stick to the solid ground. And on the way down, keep 'em peeled. For the fort. It's very, very impressive. There's an information centre. It's got a big red button. You push it, this lady tells you all about it. She does. She fills you in. Tells you everything you need to know.

Pause.

PATSY. Well that's that. I'll just fetch your fags, Wally. And it seems what's more, I'll have an informative cultural experience on the way. (*He turns to go. He turns back.*) And Mr West? If I see your bitch out there, don't worry. Dogs love me. I've been around them all my life. I know what to do.

WEST *watches him go. Long silence.* WEST *stares at* WALLY. WALLY *breathes in deep like a pearl diver, surfacing.*

WALLY. Just smell that. Eh? Smell it. (*Pause.*) I bet you sleep like a baby out here. Eh? You watch me tonight. I'll be out like a light. I won't make the count. I'll sleep like the dead.

Silence.

WALLY. What about you, Len? You sleeping well? (*Pause.*)

WEST. You been to Dartmoor before, Wally?

WALLY. Once. Camping.

WEST. As a kid?

WALLY. It was awful. All night we've got these wild horses circling the tent. I never got a wink. All around us. Just... darkness and snorting and... hooves.

WEST. Nothing sleeps out here, Wally. All the rats. The foxes. The weasels. Knackered and starving and scared. You don't sleep out here, Wally. You fall asleep out here, something creeps up and eats you. (*Beat.*) So you came.

WALLY. I course I come.

WEST. When you was late I thought whoops. Whoops Wally. Old Wally. He's let me down. He's done this. (*He turns his back.*)

WALLY. Not Wally.

WEST. Eh? (*Turns back*.) He's done this. (*Turns again. Stays turned*.)

WALLY. Not this Wally, Len.

WEST. But you come. You did. Even after what happened. (*Beat*.)

WALLY. What happened?

WEST. In your little tent, Wally. The hooves. (*Pause*.) Well, Wally. You must be devastated.

WALLY. Sorry?

WEST. No. You must be.

WALLY. Sorry. Len. What? Sorry. You've lost me.

WEST. Jerry.

WALLY. Oh. Tragic.

WEST. Awful.

WALLY. What a waste.

WEST. You must be devastated.

WALLY. Well, strictly speaking, Jerry was more your mate, Len.

WEST. Would you say?

WALLY. Strictly speaking.

WEST. Isn't that funny? I could have sworn it was more you and Jerry. I could have sworn it was more you and Jerry, rather than me and Jerry.

WALLY. Well we were the Three Musketeers, weren't we? You know… from… you know… from a distance…

WEST. The Three Musketeers.

WALLY. We were. We were the Three Stooges.

WEST. But you and Jerry, Wally? Eh? Always off in a corner. Giggling. Making each other laugh in the car.

WALLY. I'd say we were more the Three Stooges, Len. And I think each you know... each Stooge, for example, as it were... was equal. Not equal. I'm not saying that I was, you know... Of course not. Not equal. I'm not saying that... I mean you were, you know... you were... Groucho. Or whatever. The Marx Brothers. Except there was loads of them. The Three... you know... whatever. The Three... You know... Degrees. Not Degrees. That gives the wrong impression. Entirely wrong. Anyway. The Three. The Three... whatever. Exactly. That was us.

WEST. Not any more. (*Beat*.)

WALLY. No, Len. No. Not any more. (*Pause*.)

WEST. Here. Eh? You, me and Jerry? Eh? You, me and Jerry.

WALLY. Don't.

WEST. Here, do you remember...

WALLY. Yes, Len?

WEST. Talking... Do you remember – (*Starts to laugh*.)

WALLY. Yes, Mr West? (*More laughter*.) Yes, Len...?

WEST. Wales.

WALLY. Bloody hell.

WEST. Barry Island.

WALLY. Bloody hell.

WEST. Eh?

WALLY. Bloody hell.

WEST. Eh?

WALLY. Stone me. I'd clean forgot.

WEST. Me, you and Jerry. In those chalets.

WALLY. My honeymoon. With Sarah.

WEST. Sarah.

WALLY. Bloody hell. Barry. That was a party.

WEST. The whole bank holiday. No hold barred. Jerry brung that stripper.

WALLY. You brung that coloured bird.

WEST. What was her name?

WALLY. Bahar. Bazzar. Bazzer. Ree. Bazree. ReeBoz.

WEST. Me and Jerry shared a chalet. A thousand and one nights, Wally.

WALLY. An era. In bunks. All over. Scotland.

WEST. York. Cleethorpes.

WALLY. Cork. Amsterdam.

WEST. Bromsgrove. Chorleywood.

WALLY. Hove. That Portakabin in Hove. The three of us. For ten days. Waiting.

WEST. Shitting in a bucket. Next week, we're in Claridges.

WALLY. All in cummerbunds. Like it's the Oscars.

WEST. Like it never happened.

WALLY. Like it never happened. The Oscars. Exactly.

WEST. Shitting in a bucket. Bang. We're in Claridges.

WALLY. Beluga. Dom Perignon. Birds in the room.

WEST. You know what I remember. If I had to pick one, and take it with me. (*Beat*.) Highbury.

WALLY. What a day.

WEST. That day.

WALLY. What a day, Len. What a day.

WEST. In that box. It weren't the celebrities. It weren't the personalities. It was the light.

WALLY. The light.

WEST. The light. Coming right in, across the fans, onto us.

WALLY. Champagne light. Champagne.

WEST. You're in a blue suit. Jerry's in black.

WALLY. You was in a cream three-piece. You stood up the whole game at the front of the box. Ramrod straight.

WEST. That singer.

WALLY. The singer, she put her hand on your buttocks. I saw.

WEST. You don't miss a trick.

WALLY. You dirty bastard. The birds. Tongues hanging out.

WEST. How many cream suits did I have?

WALLY. It had to be ten.

WEST. Ten suits. All of white.

WALLY. No one could touch you. A lean man. All gristle. In a room. To stand a man down. Staunch. Staunch in a pinch. A flinch. Clinical. Blink. It's happened.

WEST. New York.

WALLY. Fuck me. I taught you to skate.

WEST. In Central Park. I can see us now. You, me and Jerry.

WALLY. We're on the ice.

WEST. You'd won medals.

WALLY. I was a champion skater. As a boy.

WEST. You taught us to skate.

WALLY. It was the least I could do. I walk in one day. I'm a kid. In the club.

WEST. You can't look left or right.

WALLY. I'm shaking.

WEST. Sweating.

WALLY. They're going to eat me alive.

WEST. Your heart's doing this…

WALLY. Sixteen years old.

WEST. Who puts out a hand.

WALLY. Who takes me under their wing. I'm not proud.
Without you, Mr West, I'm a smudge somewhere. On an
apron. Washing up in some caff. Fifty-pence bets. A cheap
gravestone.

WEST. The Three Musketeers.

WALLY. Exactly, Len. That's who we were. *That's* who we
were.

WEST. Who saw him jump?

WALLY. What?

Beat.

WEST. Did you see him jump, Wally? Who pulled him out?
One word to describe Jerry what would it be? Morose? Un-
stable? Haunted? Desperate? Forlorn? Who saw the body?
Did you see the body? Did you see him jump in the Thames?

WALLY. Len –

WEST. You taught him to skate. (*Pause.*)

WALLY. It's been a hard few years, Len. Everything's changed.
London is awful. You get a day off, go to the seaside, catch a
train… you can't get away. You never can. It's dark, Len.
You don't know what's next. You don't know what next.

WEST. But *you're* still here, Wally? *You're* here. *You* never
jumped in the Thames. (*Beat.*)

WALLY. Week ago, I'm sat in the doctor's, doctor in front of
me, he's holding my bollocks, I'm thinking this is it. I've got
cancer. Bollock cancer. My mobile rings. What do I do? Even
if I could, it's some weird code. They don't call back, it's a
wrong 'un. It's a wrong number. Two days later, I'm at a con-
firmation, it's on vibrate. I get out, I've got seven missed
calls. One number. Same number. Same weird, wrong number. But I've got this sixth sense. I go outside. Press redial. It
just rings and rings. I don't know it's a fucking phone box, in

some field. I'm up half the night, pressing redial, don't ask me why, I've got this sixth sense. This fucking shepherd picks up. This farmer. I'm on *The Archers*. Non capiche. Not the first word. I hang up, phone directory enquiries. It's the West Country. Somewhere on Dartmoor. My hair stands up. I just think, it must be. It must be. (*Pause*.) I've sat there for two days, by my bed, Pot Noodle, mobile charging, five chunks, just staring at it. Not moving. Two days. Waiting. Waiting. (*Pause*.) Bam. Rings once. Once. (*Beat*.) 'Hello Len.' 'Hello Wally.' 'I need help, Wally. I want to come back. I want to come home.' (*Pause*.) 'What do I do, Len? I'll do anything.' (*Pause*.) You go through Bridgetown. Two miles past. Stop. Some gate. Some red gate. Keep walking. Where? Into the darkness. Into the fucking black. (*Pause*.) You're right. I *am* here. You said come. I *came*. (*Beat*.)

Re-enter PATSY. *Pause*.

WEST. I see Patsy's back.

WALLY. Watcha, Patsy. What happened? You're all muddy again. Look at you. It's a long way down. And in the dark. You lose your bearings?

WEST. You all right, Patsy? You find your way back all right, Patsy? You stick to the path? You do what you was told?

WALLY. How'd you get on?

WEST. You see the fort? Eh? You see it this time or did you miss it again?

WALLY. Yeah... you uh... You see the fort?

WEST. Eh? Patsy? Did you see it? Did you see the fort?

PATSY. Yes. Yes. I saw it.

WEST. It's breathtaking, isn't it? Were you impressed?

Pause.

PATSY. It's nice. It's a nice fort. It must have been an extremely impressive structure in its day. Very imposing. And very atmospheric. And, I mean, I'm no expert, Mr West. But anyone can see they've built it in the wrong place. (*Beat*.)

WEST. What's that, Patsy?

WALLY. Patsy?

PATSY. Don't get me wrong. It's a cracking fort. It's just in the wrong place.

WEST. The wrong place…

WALLY. Here we go.

PATSY. I'm just saying. Yes. It's up high. Yes. It's on high land, overlooking the river, that's all textbook, textbook fort placement. See the enemy coming from miles. But they've bodged it. See, if it was me, I'd a have carried them rocks up another two hundred yards. Up to the top of the bluff… See, the land slopes sharp, and just above, just beyond all them sheep, there's a natural spur to the bluff. It's got a three hundred and sixty degree panorama and twenty feet of sheer granite to scramble up. If they'd asked me, if they'd brung me in, I'd've said whack it up there. It's a bollocks getting all that granite up there, but you'll thank me.

WALLY. How long's it been there, Patsy?

PATSY. Two-and-a-half millennia, Wally.

WALLY. And it's still standing. It's still up. Two thousand years later, the walls are still up.

PATSY. Don't get me wrong, Wally. I'm not knocking the build quality. Anyone can see that fort is supremely well realised using unquestionably durable material. I'm just saying they done it in the wrong place. (*Beat.*) See, Mr West. I done what you said, I've gone to the information centre, and I've pressed the red button, and the talking lady told me, she was very informative, she said her fort was overrun in 250 AD by marauding Picts. And I can see how they done it. They've come bundling down off that bluff. They wouldn'ta been able to've done that if the Iron Age blokes'd listened to me. You whack your fort up on the bluff, there's no bluff to attack from. You're on it. They'd still be there today. But no. They've been lazy. Cut corners. Sure enough, they've got mullered. They're yesterday's men. The sands of time have

washed over them. The rest is history. By the way, can I say
something, Mr West? Earlier, we touched upon a subject.
Namely, the subject of my mother.

WALLY. Patsy –

PATSY. It's OK, Wally. This won't take a minute. I said her
name was Rita, whereupon, in my opinion, you clearly expressed astonishment.

WALLY. Patsy –

PATSY. Please, Wally. If I may. When you done this, Wally suddenly remembered he'd left his Lamberts in the car. Now
Wally, as you outlined, loves his Lamberts. He's a pig for
'em. Can't be more than three feet from a Lambert, or he
starts sweating. I bet if we frisked Wally right now, we'd find
two, possibly three packs of Lamberts secreted about his person. (*Turns to* WALLY.) It's all right. Don't turn out your
pockets. I know why you done it. Steady the boat. Moving
right along. Well I'd like to move back if I may. To just before Wally sent me out to fetch his Lamberts. To the subject
of Rita. Rita and Wally. My mum.

WALLY. That's enough, Patsy –

PATSY. Please, Wally. This won't take a minute. When Wally
said he was with Rita, you raised an eyebrow. Expressed a
degree of astonishment. Astonishment I took it, that Wally
here would be emotionally or otherwise associated with
someone like Mum, like my mother. Like Rita.

WALLY. All right, Patsy. That's enough.

PATSY. Can I tell you a quick story, Mr West? The other day,
I'm back home at my old mum's. I'm in the tub, when the
front door opens and in comes Wally, with Mum. They've
been out, they're a bit tiddly, in the hall. I'm in the tub. They
don't know I'm there. (*Beat*.) Wally says, I heard him downstairs clear as a bell, he says, 'Rita, you are a good good
woman. Without you, I'm nothing. I'm just another stupid
old saggy dog that's going to die, rot and be forgotten.'

WALLY. When was this?

PATSY. And she says, 'Bollocks, Wally, you are an amazing
human being. You are a kind, strong, many-faceted individ-
ual, who inspires and nourishes each soul you touch.' And
Wally goes up. Big heaving sobs. He says, 'Rita, you are an
angel sent to protect me. It's cold out there. It's cold. Hold
me. Please hold me.' (*Beat*.) Now, to imagine this story, you
have to bear in mind since you last seen Rita she's got new
teeth. And she don't drink shorts no more. She's got the teeth,
some eyebrow lift what never come off. New set of Bristols.
Wally stumped for 'em. Don't get me wrong. Still, Rita em-
phatically does not scrub up. She's still got the sideburns. The
shoulders. The big goalie hands. Plus, no amount of sawing
and stitching and hammering is going to change what's un-
derneath. Time spent with Rita still often has a nightmarish
quality. Wally's had to slap her down once or twice in public.
It's worked wonders. She's made him look a right prat once
or twice. A proper clown. And you've always got to watch
her. She'll go off like a rucksack. You can't give her a yard.
Turn your back for one minute, she's in the bucket cupboard
with a broom across the door. In that Chinese restaurant. With
half the staff. About sixteen Chinamen in a broom cupboard.
They should have rung Roy Castle. But then Wally's no
church picnic. Ask the birds. Proper ogre, once the doors shut.
Right bedroom bully, once the light's off. So what I'm saying
is, I understand your reaction, Mr West. But whereas most
people would agree with us, whereas most people agree
Rita's a vicious, bitter moo you wouldn't pork with a space-
suit on, Wally here don't share the public's qualms. And the
best bit, the bonus, is I get to spend time with Wally. And time
spent with Wally is golf, mate. It's pure golf. On the way over
here, he's pulled the car over, he looked me in the eye and
he's said, 'I don't want you to think I'm soppy. 'I'm not being
bent or nothing but I love you, Patsy.'

WALLY. Steady.

PATSY. 'I do. And I'll look after you.'

WALLY. Steady the bus.

PATSY. 'And I'm not being bent, but I love that Mr West. That
Len – ' he said. Look. He's blushing now, like a woman, like

a prat, but he said it, on the M5. 'It don't matter what he's done. Why he's out in the cold. I'd go to the moon for that man. To the moon.' (*Beat*.) I just want to say... Thank you, Wally. Some fathers wouldn't. Some would just leave you in the dark. Not you, Wally. And also to say, and *I'm* not being bent, but ditto. I love you too. And you love Mr West. And Mr West, I don't doubt, you know, eh? Eh? I bet? Eh? You know? Eh? So here we are. Eh? Men who love each other, but who are not benders. Here's your Lamberts, Wally.

He gives them to him. Long silence.

WEST. Why don't we sit down? Eh? Patsy. Come in. Come in. Come and sit down.

PATSY *sits in the armchair. The others stay standing.*

You want some more wine, Wally?

WALLY. Lovely. Lovely drop.

WEST. Scotch, Patsy?

PATSY. I won't if it's all the same, Mr West.

WEST. You sure? There's plenty.

PATSY. It's extremely kind. No.

Pause.

WEST. I want to apologise.

PATSY. What?

WEST. I didn't mean to cast aspersions. I'm sorry if I seemed rude. I've been out of the loop. I'm catching up.

PATSY. I understand, Mr West.

WEST. The last thing in the world I want to do is offend you. Not when we've just met.

PATSY. Thank you, Mr West.

WEST. I hope there's no hard feelings.

PATSY. None whatsoever.

WEST. Are you sure?

PATSY. Certain.

WEST. Good. Have we cleared that up?

PATSY. I believe we have.

WEST. Good. Because I need to clear something up too. Something from earlier. Something you said.

Silence.

PATSY. Yes, Mr West. (*Pause.*)

WEST. It's about the fort.

PATSY. The fort.

WALLY. The fort.

WEST. Yes. The fort. Earlier, I said when you're on the way down, Patsy, why don't you stop and take a look at the fort. And you said you would. And you did. And when you come back, you said in your opinion, it's in the wrong place. (*Beat.*)

PATSY. Yes, Mr West.

WEST. It's in the wrong place.

PATSY. Yes.

WEST. That's what you think.

PATSY. Well... Yes.

WEST. You're sure?

PATSY. Well... Yes.

WEST. You're absolutely one hundred per cent certain that that fort is in the wrong place? (*Pause.*)

PATSY. Well. Mr West. If you stood on my chest. I hope I haven't offended you. I'm sorry if I have. I certainly didn't mean to. I mean. At the end of the day. It's a fort. (*Pause.*)

WEST. You said you went to the information centre.

PATSY. Yes, Mr West.

WEST. You pressed the big red button. You got the speaking lady.

PATSY. That's right, Mr West.

WEST. You listened to what she had to say. About the fort.

PATSY. Well yes, Mr West. You said to. So I did...

WEST. You listened to her. Like I said.

PATSY. Yes, Mr West. Like you told me to. (*Pause*.)

WEST. What year was the fort built? (*Beat*.) When was the fort built, Patsy?

PATSY. Let's see. I think she said circa 600 BC.

WEST. 600 BC.

PATSY. Yes. Wait. No.

WEST. Yes. Wait. No.

PATSY. I'm not sure.

WEST. You're not sure.

PATSY. It depends what you mean.

WEST. It's a simple question. When was the fort built?

PATSY. Well. It's tricky actually. See, the present Iron Age fort was built in 600 BC. But the speaking lady said that fort's built on the foundations of an older fort, which dates back to Mesolithic times. That's approximately 6000 BC. So it depends.

WEST. How big was the fort? What were the fort's dimensions?

PATSY. Well. The main keep is eighty yards in diameter. So it covers roughly one acre in modern terms.

WEST. What did the fort contain?

PATSY. Lots of things.

WEST. Like what?

PATSY. A granary. A smithy. An earthwatch, the chieftain's house and the citizens' dwellings.

WEST. How many dwellings?

PATSY. Twenty-five.

WEST. How big were the dwellings?

PATSY. Each dwelling was twelve to fifteen feet in diameter.

WEST. When they dug it up. What were the main archeological finds?

PATSY. Nothing special. Usual stuff. Swords, spears, axes, fish hooks. Clay pots. Arrow-heads.

WEST. Nothing special.

PATSY. What do you mean? Oh. Yes. There was one thing.

WEST. What?

PATSY. A single white-flint hand axe of Iron Age workmanship.

WEST. What's Dartmoor made out of?

PATSY. Granite. Granite on molten magma.

WEST. When did tin mining begin in the area?

PATSY. The Bronze Age. What plant covers sixty per cent of Dartmoor?

WEST. Heather.

PATSY. Which way does the entrance of the fort face?

WEST. South. Towards?

PATSY. Arrowfleet. Why?

WEST. The grazing grounds. So it overlooks the grazing grounds. What stands to the west?

PATSY. A burial mound. A megalithic graveyard.

WEST. What stands to the east…?

PATSY. To the east is a stone circle. How big is it?

WEST. Eighty feet across. How many stones?

PATSY. Sixteen granite stones. How big are the stones?

WEST. Between ten and thirteen feet high.

PATSY. How heavy are the stones?

WEST. Smallest is three tons.

PATSY. The biggest is twelve tons.

WEST. What was it used for? What was the stone circle used for? (*Pause.*) What was the stone circle used for?

PATSY. I... (*Pause.*) Hang on. (*Pause.*) Wait...

Pause.

WEST. When did you decide to come? (*Pause.*) How long did you think about it? Have you got the stomach for this, Patsy? Not just the stomach. The kidneys. The lungs. The neck. The teeth. The skill. The knowledge. In your bones. In your fingernails. In your teeth. It's not just front. Muscle and front. Nerve and bluster. What are you made of, Patsy? What are you made of?

Silence.

PATSY. Sacrifice. (*Pause.*) The stone circle was used for sacrifice. (*Beat.*) Human sacrifice.

Silence. PATSY*'s nose starts to bleed.*

WALLY. Patsy –

PATSY. It's all right.

WALLY. I'm sorry, Mr West. Patsy.

PATSY. I said... I said it's... I... I get... I got... I get these... It's nothing... I... It's...

He sits there, letting it bleed.

WEST. It's your turn, Patsy. It's your go.

PATSY *wipes his nose. He has blood on his shirt. Silence.*

PATSY. Who's the girl? (*Pause*.) The one upstairs.

WALLY. What? (*Pause*.)

PATSY. Who is she?

WALLY. What you talking about, Patsy? You not been upstairs.

PATSY. I know. But she's up there. I saw her. Coming back up the path. She's in the window. Looking out. Not moving. Just staring down. I waved to her. Who is she? Who's the girl?

Silence.

Blackout.

End of Act One.

ACT TWO

The dead of winter. The previous year.

The farmhouse is even more desolate and derelict. Many floor-boards are broken. Someone has had a bonfire in the middle of the room. Rats dart about.

WEST *stands motionless to one side. He is filthy, cold, as if he has been sleeping rough for months.*

Enter DRAYCOTT *from the back.*

DRAYCOTT. It's just like I said, Mister. You're a lucky man.

> *Pause.* DRAYCOTT *removes something wrapped in grease-proof paper from his pocket. He unwraps it.*

> I've been over Chagford. They love me at that butcher's. Sniff that. Get the beauty of it. That's fresh killed, that is. That was snuffling around only this morning. You had heart? He's good gear. Good for the blood. And the other. I don't mind sharing. And you look like you could use a feed. So what do you say? Are you in? (*He breaks sachets of salt and pepper.*)

WEST. Thank you.

DRAYCOTT. Pig's the best. And this is fresh. You won't get finer in Buckingham Palace. I've cooked all over the West Country. Pubs. Rugby clubs. Newton Abbot Racecourse. I once cooked for eighty-six estate agents. A good fresh piece, get the pan hot. Onions, carrot, bit of butter. You wouldn't have an onion on your person, have you?

WEST. No.

DRAYCOTT. A carrot?

WEST. No.

DRAYCOTT. Butter? (*Beat.*) Not to worry. (*He spits in the pan, tosses the hearts in, whole.*) Oh yes, you're very lucky I was in. I'm usually out, on my rounds. Mr Darling kills on Mondays. So, I'm in there early, acting the nag. Jabber away, touch the meat, pick up the knives. They get jumpy, Hey Preston, they bung me a trotter. A piece of liver. A heart or two just to piss off. I pop up all over. Princetown. Two Bridges. Dartmeet. Fruit shops are good. There's a baker in Ashburton who'll pay me two quid just to fuck off. Newsagents. Walk in. Start gibbering. End of the world. That's a Yorkie. Couple bags of crisps. Just once a fortnight, mind. You can't take the piss. But the baker's a soft touch. Try it. Be my guest. You got to time it, see. Watch for a hour or two, wait till they're chocker, lunchtime's good, right when they're rushed off their feet, then bundle in, start licking the walls. Works every time. But don't go in Darling's. That's mine. You hear? I don't want to hear you've been in Darling's. I hear you've been bothering Mr Darling, I'll be on the warpath. I'm serious. You set foot near the place, I'll have your guts. In fact I've made a decision. It's best you steer clear of Chagford altogether. Stay back. They know me over there. (*Beat.*) Here. Do you know what I thought when I saw you? Can I? I said to myself, there is a capital man. He's from up there. The capital. A mile off. They stand different, Londoners. He's seen it. He's been around it. He's been in airports all over the world. You wouldn't think to look at him, but I can see it. I can see through things. And look closer. He's got good hair, also. And teeth. It's all about the teeth and the hair, when you get down to it. (*Pause.*) What was I saying? What was I just saying when I come in? What was I talking about?

WEST. Badgers.

DRAYCOTT. Was I? Really?

WEST. Yes.

DRAYCOTT. Why?

WEST. I don't know. (*Pause.*)

DRAYCOTT. Exactly. Badgers. Bastards. Never mess with a badger. I had a fight with a badger once. I'm coming home from The Feathers, full moon it was, and I'm taking a short-cut across Fletcher's Field. I stop in this clearing and there he is. Big lad. Stripy. I've seen him before. I'm good with faces. I'm a demon. Previous June I've lugged a tree trunk at him. Now he's back. And he's brung two mates. Now I'm a good talker, I could talk my way out of most things, but they're not having it. Their backs are up. You can smell it coming. I got no choice. So I stand as big as I can, and I bellows, 'Right. Let's have it you stripy cunts.' Big mistake. He's on me in a flash. And his chums. I was in bed for a month. Lost five pints of blood to it. And two toes. They should stamp them out. But they better do the lot, 'cause I'm here to tell you, the badger bears a grudge. (*Beat.*) You get to know the ropes, you'll like it down here. But steer clear of Chagford. And Ashburton. Absolute shithole. Last June I've gone over there to see if I could get a game. Cricket this is. I know the skipper. He's an old friend. Runs Specsavers in Ashburton. All right Skip, any chance of a knockaround? Nothing doing. Full up, he says. Fair enough. Week later, I'm strolling in the park and I see they're playing. The cricketeers. So I go over and I cannot believe my fucking eyes. (*Beat.*) They've got a girl at short midwicket. Ten years old. I've marched straight out to the wicket and had it out with the skipper. I've not been rude. I've got a case. That skipper's gone out of his way to humiliate a man who could put on thirty or forty without breaking a sweat. In the end, they called the police. I had the last laugh. By the time they got me off it was chucking it down. I showed them. And I never left it at that. All season, every home game, I'm there, on the boundary, when this skipper pads up, I've got the *Telegraph* rolled up... 'Oy, you fat bender.' 'You great big goggle-eyed cunt.' Now that's not me. Normally. And whoever it was chucked a breeze-block through Specsavers, that weren't me neither. I walked on that one. Get some CCTV, you bastards. Pay your fucking taxes. They're all vicious, vicious people, over Ashburton. Which is odd because it's the drier side of the moor. Here we go. Here we go.

WEST. What?

A plane tears over, shaking the walls.

DRAYCOTT. Every fifteen minutes. I went down there, to the
base to complain. Turns out the bloke on the desk, he can't
do nothing about it. It's a trig point, he says. Says all the
planes, the RAF, choppers, fighters, bombers, they roar
out over the forest and turn left over the fort. It's a landmark,
see. Trig point. We're losing the war, mate, meanwhile
you're back home, scaring the shit out of sheep. Are you all
right? You look like you're shivering. You want to get near
this warm, mate. You want to come a bit closer.

WEST. Who owns it?

DRAYCOTT. Who owns what?

WEST. This house.

DRAYCOTT. What you talking about it? That's cheek, that is.
That's royal cheek. *I* own it, mate. This house is *mine*.
You're my guest. You're enjoying my hospitality. What did
you think this was?

WEST. I'm sorry.

DRAYCOTT. You wouldn't believe it but when I first got here
this place was crammed full of filthy stinking animals. Rats.
Dogs. Weasels. Vagrants. The Unemployed. Deviants. Desert-
ers. The Depressed. I didn't hang about. I used my military
training. We're getting there. This'll be a home again. Slowly
slowly, catchee monkee. (*He takes the frying pan off.*) That's
it. Not a moment more. Here. Get the beauty of it. Smell that.
Smell that. (*He does.*) Nope, I've fucked it. I've burned him.
He's useless he is. Absolutely pointless. You need butter. And
onions. And you sorely need that carrot. Not to worry. (*He
tosses it away.*) I've got back-up. (*He whips out two bags of
crisps.*) Smoky Bacon or Farmhouse Cheddar? Here you go.
(*Throws one.*) You know I could use a man like you.

WEST. How?

DRAYCOTT. Help me do this place up. A lick of paint here and
there. Fix that chair. Put in units. Get this place back to glory.
I'll strike you a bargain. I know someone with access to
whitewash. And I know another fellow's got a mattress. It's
practically new. You give me a hand, tarting her up, keeping

the riffraff back, it's yours. You and me could go over there
and bring it back. It's about six miles. It's a two-man job. We
could lick this place into shape. What do you say? You and
me. Are you in? (*Pause.*)

Enter a young girl, LUE. *Young. Small. Icicle-thin. Lipstick.
A small army rucksack on her back. In a mac, with high
heels, holding two old plastic shopping bags in one hand,
and a hat box in the other, tied up with bailing twine.*

Pause. Another plane streaks over.

Oh here we go. Here we go. Ssh. Hang on. You'll like this.
This is a good laugh. Hang about. (*He goes over.*) Well well
well. How is Her Majesty? Did she pass the night pleasantly?
No disturbances? No bad dreams? (*He bows low.*) May I
offer my lowly salutations and enquire where we have passed
this crisp, fine day? Where have you been these three days
hence? And pray tell, what's the capital of Russia? Where's
the English Channel? Who plays centre-half for Arsenal?
What's two plus two? How many fingers am I holding up?
Who wrote Beethoven's Fifth?

Silence. She doesn't react.

Here look. Look. Here look. Madam has new shoes. And
handsome they are too, with fine stitching. Pray tell, hast
thou been to Okehampton, for a spot of shoplifting? Or in the
car park of Lidl's, checking car doors. Or round the back of
the sport centre on your hands and knees.

He laughs. He rounds on her.

I heard you banging about down here last night. Good folk
are trying to sleep. I sent you out for firewood, you swan
back in three days later with a new coat. New shoes. Where's
the fuel, you dozy slut? Eh? You been over Nero's, aintch
you? Stuffing your face with pills. Catching stuff, bringing it
back. I tell you what, you need pills, love. Some for your
head and some for downstairs. And some to open that gob. I
tell you, it tries you, Mister. And I'm a patient soul. But day
in, day out. (*He looks to* WEST.) Watch this.

He mimics a spastic. Putting on a spastic voice.

'I've been over Okehampton. I've been shagging squaddies.
They been buying me coats. I been riding with the Lord
Mayor with sixteen stallions. I been to the finest parts of the
world. I got ladies who run my bath.' (*He stops and laughs*.)
Have a go. Ask her anything? Go on. Eh? Your Majesty. Can
you do this? Follow along. Follow along.

He rubs his stomach and pats his head.

Can you do this?

He makes a fucking gesture.

I tell you… someone's dropped her on her head. Or they
bloody should.

He stands right in front of her.

Where's Mummy and Daddy? Eh? Did you get lost in the su-
permarket? Where's Mummy? Where's my mummy? Last
winter it was, she shows up in the middle of the afternoon in
her scundies. I swear. It's nine below. She was blue. Been
out on the moor for days. Down the barracks no doubt. Came
back stinking like a bag of whelks. (*Winks*.) What's the capital of Persia? (*To* WEST.) Have a go. She won't mind. But
watch your stuff. You think she bought that coat. Nothing
doing. What you got in your bag, Missus? Eh? Sticky fingers. She has a bath once in a blue moon. If you're gonna get
hold of her you've got to time it right. Then she'll suck you
off for a conker. I've never known the like.

He rounds on her again.

You better start pulling your weight or you're out of here.
And I'll see to it. Contribute. Muck in. I don't mind how.
There's more than one way to skin a cat, eh? Eh?

He laughs. He takes WEST *aside.*

Here. Are you ready? I've got half a bottle of Scotch up-
stairs. She's partial. She's thirsty, if you know what I mean.
What do you say, eh? Here's the play. You keep her talking,
I'll get the juice, get it down her, Hey Preston. You won't
believe it. Half a mo. Just keep her busy. This is the one, eh?
Watch this. (*He heads off*.) I won't be a minute, princess,

I'm just popping upstairs to see to the plumbing. Talk amongst yourselves.

He goes upstairs leaving the two of them together. Silence.

WEST *sits with his crisps.* LUE *puts her bags down and goes to the cupboard. She takes out some Ribena. She makes herself a Ribena. She drinks it. She goes to her bag. Upwraps a Yorkie. Eats a couple of squares. They keep catching each other's eyes. Silence.*

Sheep. WEST *can't stand it any longer.*

LUE. Who are you?

WEST. No one.

LUE. You his friend?

WEST. I thought you never spoke.

LUE. Who said I never spoke?

WEST. He said you said...

LUE. I never said nothing.

WEST. No but... he said... he said you never spoke.

LUE. Of course I speak. I just don't speak to him.

WEST. Why not?

LUE. It goes without saying. Where'd you meet him?

WEST. Today.

LUE. Where was he?

WEST. In a field.

LUE. That's him. A word of warning. You know the way most people have got a sweet side? He hasn't. (*Beat.*) He's all right. He's old, in'e? He be lucky he makes it through the winter. He cries in his sleep. And he knitted me a scarf once. He's a good knitter. You wouldn't think it, but he can really knit.

WEST. Why don't you talk to him?

LUE. I used to. It didn't pan out. So I've sent him to Coventry. And it's not far enough. He tell his story?

WEST. About the badger.

LUE. Not the badger. How he owns this place.

WEST. Yes.

LUE. Embarassing, isn't it? Oh yes. He's got a dozen properties in the area. He's got a portfolio. He commutes between here and his private island.

A plane tears over.

That's him now. He's done one. He's gone to stink up somewhere else. Why are your hands shaking?

Beat.

LUE. You're from London, aren't you?

WEST. What?

LUE. I know you. I've seen you before. (*Beat.*) Lots of times…

WEST. Where?

LUE. Lot's of times. Plymouth. Last spring. You was in the hostel. On Kerry Road. You was in front of me in the queue. They asked you who you was and you said you was from London. You said you was in business. Then over Hexworthy Bridge, first week of August… Out on the moor. You was trying to skin a rabbit. Then a week later, further up river, you was washing your feet on the bank. You had a little camp. Then in Okehampton a month ago. You were drunk out your mind. Screaming at the shoppers. Foaming at the mouth. They called the police but you ran. You ran off. That was you, that was. Then I saw you yesterday.

WEST. Where?

LUE. In the fort. You were sitting there. On the parapet. You was crying, muttering to yourself. I come close but I couldn't hear you. You looked frozen. I went off, into Okehampton. To the pictures, come back and you was still there. You'd stopped gibbering. You was just looking down at the land below as it went dark. Stock-still. Staring. And when I looked out the next morning, you was gone.

Pause.

WEST. I've seen you too.

LUE. I don't doubt it. I'm around.

WEST. About a month ago. On a bus in Ashburton. You were alone. Your face was cut. You had argument with the driver. He stopped the bus and chucked you off.

LUE. Have you been abroad?

WEST. What? Yeah. I've been abroad.

LUE. Where've you been?

WEST. Lots of places.

LUE. Have you got a passport?

WEST. Not on me.

LUE. All you've got on you's dirt, mate. I'm saying before. In London. When you was a business man. It stands to reason. You went abroad, you had a passport. Did you have a passport?

WEST. Yes.

LUE. Did you fill out the form?

WEST. What?

LUE. What colour was it?

WEST. What?

LUE. What colour was it?

WEST. I don't remember.

LUE. Was it blue?

WEST. I don't remember what colour it was.

LUE. How big was it? How many pages? Did it fold out, like this?

WEST. I can't…

LUE. What? You can't what?

WEST. It was a long time ago. What's the matter?

LUE. I need help.

WEST. What you talking about?

LUE. Filling out forms. A form. I'm going away. I'm going
    abroad.

WEST. Where?

LUE. I got everything else. I've got sun cream. And a hat. And
    sunglasses. And a towel. And a bikini. And a book. I just
    need to do the form. I just need to fill it out. Get someone to
    sign it. Then I need to borrow forty pound. For the passport
    application. Then there's the stamp. Then I need two hundred
    pounds for the flight. That's the cost of the flight from Exeter
    Airport. Also, I've got to get to Exeter, so I need bus fare.
    What do you say?

WEST. I can't help you.

LUE. Why not?

WEST. I can't… I… I haven't got any money.

LUE. You said you was a businessman.

WEST. So what?

LUE (*beat*). Here. (*She takes out a form.*) This isn't the form.
    This is the form you need to fill out the form. The form form
    is safe. The form form's upstairs. This is the pre-form. The
    other one. The orange one. Don't touch it. Your hands are
    filthy. You smudge it, we're buggered. Here look. (*She reads.*)
    'Section One. Form C1. A. One. Please keep these Notes until
    you receive your passport. Note 1a, subsection one – Birth
    after 31 December 1982 in the United Kingdom. Tick 'Yes' if
    you were born after 31 December 1982 in the United King-
    dom, or if you entered the country on or before December 31
    1989, or after July 1 1992, unless a) you were already a tem-
    porary citizen in which case refer to note 2a, subsection

seven…' And I speak English. That's their opener. That's
their warm-up. I mean, that's that. I'm staying put. I ain't
going nowhere, am I? Wait for it. (*She searches.*) This is the
bit. Where is it? (*Reads.*) 'Note 5a, section three.' No, that's
not it. Where is it? Here you go. (*Reads.*) 'Section 12a, sub-
section 2ii should be signed by a British citizen, or other
Commonwealth citizen, who is a Member of Parliament, Jus-
tice of the Peace, Minister of Religion, Established Civil Ser-
vant, or… here we go… professionally qualified person in the
community, e.g. Businessman, Doctor, blah blah blah, or a
person of similar standing.' See? I need someone from the
community. Someone they trust. Someone of standing. Now I
was thinking, if he was a businessman, or say, or a doctor,
then he can do it. Because I figure, he's not been out here
long. They probably don't know yet. The government. They
probably don't know that he's gibbering in Okehampton Mar-
ket. What do you reckon? What do you say?

WEST. I can't help you.

LUE. What?

WEST. I can't help you.

LUE. Why not?

WEST. I can't help you… I've…

LUE. I just need you to sign my photo. Sign the form. Read the
notes. Say who you are. Vouch for me. I've got everything
else. You help me, I won't forget it. You help me, that's that.
I'm out of here. You can have my room. You won't freeze to
death, out there in your fort. What do you say? Eh? What do
you say?

WEST. I can't help you.

LUE. Why not? Why can't you?

WEST. Because I'm… I'm not the man you're looking for. I'm
not from the community.

LUE. You said you was in business.

WEST. No I never…

LUE. You did. I heard you. You said you was. You said you was in business. Don't lie to me. Don't fob me off. I heard you. You said you was in business. A businessman. I need a businessman. Someone from the community. That's you. Are you from the community? Are you from the community?

WEST. I'm not a businessman. I'm not a doctor. I'm not from the community.

LUE. Well then who are you? (*Beat.*)

WEST. I'm…

LUE. Who are you? Eh? Who are you? Who are you?

WEST (*loud*). I'M NOT FROM THE COMMUNITY! OK? I'm not a business… I'm not a fucking businessman… I'm… I'm not… I'm not from the community… (*Pause.*) I just… I fell asleep.

LUE. What? (*Pause.*)

WEST. I fell asleep. (*Pause.*) I… I was… I was… watching this flat. For five days. I've not slept. For weeks. I was… I was tired. I was… I just needed to… But I had to watch this… I'm sat in this car… And I was so tired. I just… I just… I just… I just…

LUE. What?

WEST. I fell asleep. I must have… I… I must. I… I… (*Pause.*) I drove back… back to London. I drove… and… They… they… they… shut me in a room. (*Beat.*) They gave me gin. Filled me up with… Then these blokes come in. These two… They snapped my thumbs. They broke my thumbs. They broke my foot… with a sledgehammer. They burned me. Kettles of water with… with sugar in, so it sticks. They… kicked me in the bollocks till they… till they was pumpkins… Swallow petrol. Bleach. Piss. Spunk. For days. 'Don't fall asleep, Len. Don't doze off. You dozy cunt. Dozy baby.' Singing lullabies. Over and over.

Pause.

You think that's horrible. I've done it. I've done it myself. And worse. In rooms. To… To other people. You don't

know 'em. You just... they've... they've done... A decision's been... you know... It's... It's... (*Pause.*) I can't help
you. I'm not a businessman. I'm not... I'm not from the
community.

Silence.

LUE (*putting the form away*). I'm sorry. It wasn't you I saw.
It was someone else. I thought you was someone else.

She gathers her things and heads upstairs.

WEST. Look –

LUE. I'm sorry. I won't keep you.

WEST. Look. I'll...

LUE. I'm sorry. Forget it.

WEST. No, look –

LUE. Just forget it. I'll find someone...

WEST. Look... I'll look at... I'll look at it. I'll... your form. I'll
take a look at it. You... you show me it, I might be able to...
I might...

Silence.

LUE. It won't be for free. I'll give you something.

WEST. What?

LUE. I'll pay you. I haven't got money, but I'll pay you.

WEST. Look, I don't want nothing.

LUE. Listen –

WEST. I don't need nothing. I just...

LUE. Hang on –

WEST. I don'. Really. Please.

LUE. You don't know what it is yet. How do you know you
don't want it if you don't know what it is?

WEST. Look –

LUE. You don't know what I'm offering. (*She holds up the hat box*.)

WEST. What's that?

Pause.

LUE. I found it. Out on the moor. If you help me, you can have it.

WEST. What is it?

LUE. You help me, it's yours. If you help me… She's yours.

WEST. She?

LUE. She's only small. Just been born. Two, three days old. You'll have to look after her. If you help me, you can have her. (*Pause*.) It's the room at the end. Overlooking the fort. Come when it's dark. Will you help me?

Pause.

Re-enter DRAYCOTT, *from upstairs.*

DRAYCOTT. Here we go. I keep for emergencies. I rub it on my chest when I've got the flu. Go on then. Cowboy-style. You not thirsty, love? Don't stand on ceremony.

LUE *drinks it down.*

There we go.

She drinks it down.

One more.

She drinks it down. She finishes the whole bottle. Gives it back to him, walks up to WEST. *Silence.*

WEST (*nods*). Yes.

LUE. Come when it's dark.

She turns. And leaves.

DRAYCOTT. What? What did she say? Oy. You talking now? Where you going, you filthy twizzler? Come back, you tart. Come back. We ain't finished.

She's gone.

She'll pay for that. That's good Scotch, that is. She owes me... the fucking neck. The brass... fuckin'... She'll pay for that. She knows n' all. She'll pay. When she's asleep. She'll pay sorely. (*Pause.*) What did she say, Mister? Just then. What did she say? What did that little cat say?

WEST. She said...

DRAYCOTT. The minx. That little shag, what did she say?

WEST. She said she's seen me before.

DRAYCOTT. What? What's that lying tart on about? She's seen you before? Come off it. A man like you. A tart like that. Come off it.

WEST. She said she's seen me before. (*Beat.*) And I've seen you before.

DRAYCOTT. What you on about? Where?

WEST. Here. In this house.

DRAYCOTT. What you talking about? I never saw you here.

WEST. Yes you did. A few days ago. Monday it was. We sat in here. We played gin rummy.

DRAYCOTT. Gin rummy?

WEST. We played all evening. Gin. The cards are in that drawer over there.

DRAYCOTT. I never seen you before, Mister. I'm a demon with faces. And I'd remember a game of gin. No danger. You owe me for the crisps. I... I show you human... I show you kindness. And the... and the... don't go into Chagford. And you can forget the mattress. And you owe me for the crisps. Go on. Get out of it. I changed my mind. I want you out of here. You hear me? Get out. Get out of it. Get out.

WEST. We sat in this room. A week ago. We played gin. We were drinking whisky. My glass. Every time it was empty. You filled it up. Just before dawn, I went outside, to piss.

When I came back in, you were going through my bag. Rifling through it. You found something. I walked across the room, and took it from you. I told you who I was. I told you everything. (*Beat.*) The sun came up. It started to snow.

He regards DRAYCOTT.

Silence.

Blackout.

End of Act Two.

ACT THREE

The house as in Act One. The next morning. Sheep.

Enter PATSY *from upstairs. Freezing. He still has blood on his shirt. He looks around the place. He goes in the back and runs a tap. Comes back, wringing the shirt out. He spots the mangle. Goes over. He has no idea how to work it. He puts the shirt in. Starts winding. It gets stuck. He tries to pull it out and rips it in half. He finds a coat on the back of the door. He puts it on. He does star jumps to warm himself. Does ten press-ups. Another ten. He plays a few notes on the piano. It's out of tune. He lights a cigarette. He stops. Looks up the stairs. We can't see at what.*

PATSY. Hello there. I'm... I'm Patsy. (*Pause. He indicates the cigarette.*) I was just having my breakfast. You want one? (*Pause.*) Eh? You want a Benson then? Come on. (*Pause.*) Come on. That's it. You want one. You do, don't you? Come on then. Don't worry. I won't bite.

Enter LUE, *from upstairs.*

There we go. There we go.

He offers the packet. Slowly she takes one. She puts it in her pocket.

I saw you yesterday from the window. The one what waved. I was coming up the path last night, in the dark and I've looked up and... you saw me. Did you see me? On the path? I thought you did. Did you?

LUE. That's not your coat.

PATSY. Oh. Right. I had nosebleed. I get them sometimes... when uh... I washed my shirt and... well. You're in that end room, aren't you? Overlooks the fort. I'm next door. We're neighbours, you and me. How's your room? Is it warm? Mine's not. Mine's got no window. Someone's smashed it. And before you ask, it was a trifle. Truth is I've not slept.

But then I never slept yesterday. Or the day before. I've not slept for weeks. Search me. When I do sleep, it's worse. But then I don't need much, me. Never did. How's your bed? Is it warm? I've not got a bed. I've got a pile of old rubbish. I've drawn the short straw. (*Pause*.) We come down to visit a friend. Mr West. Spend some time. Catch up. (*Beat*.) So are and him, you know… So are you and him, you know…

LUE. He's my friend.

PATSY. Oh. I see.

LUE. We talk to each other. He's got this little dog I gave him. We all sit together by that fire, or wherever, in my room. (*Pause*.) But now the dog's run off. She's been gone for days. So you're his friend too?

PATSY. Strictly speaking, I'm a friend of a friend. Stricter speaking, I'm the stepson of a friend. But actually I'm not.

LUE. So why did you come?

PATSY. See, that's just it. I can't tell you. See, the way it works, I'm in bed, my mobile rings. Someone says, 'Patsy, they'll pick you up outside the Costcutters at ten o'clock. Don't bring nothing.' A toothbrush. A credit card. (*Pause*.) You don't ask questions. You don't want to put a foot wrong. Not one foot. I'm not bothered. I'll go anywhere.

LUE. Have you been abroad?

PATSY. Once or twice.

LUE. Where have you been?

PATSY. Loads of places.

LUE. Holidays?

PATSY. Yes.

LUE. Business trips?

PATSY. One or two.

LUE. I'm going abroad. I've got my passport.

PATSY. That's nice. Where you going? Somewhere nice? Somewhere hot.

LUE. That's right. Somewhere where it's hot all year. All summer, all winter.

PATSY. Lovely.

LUE. That's where I'm going. That's where I'm off to.

PATSY. Sounds lovely.

LUE. Yeah. But I can't go yet. See, my suitcase is broken. I bought this suitcase and it's cheap. It's a piece of crap. I put all my stuff in it, and the strap's bust. So I can't go yet. I've got to get a new suitcase. Then that's that. I'm off. Well it was nice to meet you.

PATSY. Likewise.

LUE. Goodbye.

Beat.

PATSY. Did you see me?

LUE. When?

PATSY. Last night. When you were at the window. When I waved to you. You were looking right at me. Did you see me?

Silence.

LUE. I suppose I must have.

PATSY. What do you mean?

LUE. I mean, I must have, mustn't I? Because I dreamt about you.

PATSY. What?

LUE. I dreamt about you last night. You were in my dream. It was definitely you. I can see you now.

PATSY. What happened?

LUE. I was walking down the path, down to the road. It was just getting light. And it was freezing cold, so I took the shortcut through the fort. I went into the main part. The main hall it is. The banqesting hall. Where they had the banquets. And it was freezing cold, and it was snowing. And there you was.

PATSY. What was I doing?

LUE. You was sitting on the parapet. You was staring out over the land below. You were stock-still. I went over, and when I got close, I touched your shoulder. You were frozen solid. Like a statue. Cold as stone.

PATSY. What did you do?

LUE. What could I do? I left you there.

PATSY. You left me?

LUE. Yes. But before I left you. I did something.

PATSY. What? What did you do? What did you do?

LUE. I kissed your cheek. It was frozen. But then... you opened your eyes. And you turned to me and smiled. And the next morning, I come out, and you were gone. Where you'd been there was just ripped clothes and blood. And bones.

Pause. Enter WEST.

WEST. Morning, Patsy.

PATSY. Morning, Mr West.

WEST. You sleep well?

PATSY. Not that well as it happens. We were just... we were just... you know... talking.

WEST. Oh yes. What about? (*Beat.*)

PATSY. Holidays.

WEST. Holidays. (*Pause.*)

PATSY. So where's this suitcase?

LUE. What?

PATSY. Your suitcase. You said it's broke. The buckle's broke. Perhaps I could take a look at it?

LUE. You sure?

PATSY. Why not?

LUE. I don't know. I can't give you nothing.

PATSY. I don't want nothing. It's just a buckle. Where is it? Where's the suitcase? I'll take a look at it.

Pause.

LUE. It's upstairs.

PATSY. We won't be a moment, Mr West.

PATSY *nods. They go upstairs.* WEST *looks up the stairs, fixed. Pause. Enter* WALLY *from outside. Behind him.*

WALLY. Up with the lark. Same as always. I've been for a walk. Bitter, it is. The ground's froze solid. You sleep well, Len?

WEST (*without turning*). You sleep well, Wally?

WALLY. Country air, isn't it? A right tonic. It was just like I said it would be. I've gone out sparko. I've woke up, it's like I've had a thousand nights' kip.

WEST (*up the stairs*). Where'd you walk then?

WALLY. I've just set off. I've gone for a ramble, me. The funny thing is, Len...

WEST. What's that?

WALLY. Call me a berk. Call me a tonk. I still can't find that blessed fort. I've looked everywhere. I'm thinking, 'Come on, Coker, it must be round here somewhere.' I've got completely lost. I end up down by this river. It's froze solid. I've stepped out on it and you know what's happened? Nothing. It's held my weight. I pushed off and I've slid clean across it. Did I tell you I used to skate as a kid? At Queensway. I've won medals.

WEST. Really, Wally?

WALLY. It's true. It's like riding a bicycle. I've skated clean down the river. Like a kid. Over the rocks. On my soles. By the way, there's good news.

WEST. What's that then?

WALLY. The car. Rita's car. Her little two-seater. I got Rita's two-seater out that ditch. Out that bog. See, with the freeze, with the temperature dropped, the earth's froze. I got the

wheels to bite. I got traction, didn't I? I floored it, she come
flying out. Now she's standing on the road. Ready to go.

WEST. You're back in business.

WALLY. We are. We are. We're ready to rock…

WEST. This time in the morning, not too much traffic.

WALLY. A following wind. We'll be home in no time. (*Pause*.)
Is Patsy up?

WEST. He's upstairs.

WALLY. The dozy git. Is he asleep?

WEST. He didn't sleep.

WALLY. Did he not? That's a shame. Now he'll be grumpy all
the way home. (*Pause*.) I was just thinking, Len. Can I give
you a lift?

WEST. What?

WALLY. Can I give you a lift somewhere?

WEST. What do you mean?

WALLY. I just thought. The engine's running. Maybe I could
give you a lift somewhere.

WEST. Where?

WALLY. Well, where do you want to go? Into town? Some-
where I can drop you. Ashburton. Exeter. Bristol. Swindon.
Salisbury. Newbury. Reading. Home. (*Pause*.) It's been
a while, Len. You could go up West. You could see a show.
You could have dinner. Like a human. What do you say?
Do you want a lift, Len? (*Pause*.)

WEST. I thought you was a two-seater.

WALLY. We are. A two-seater. Rita's little two-seater. (*Pause*.)

WEST. What do I have to do? (*Pause*.)

WALLY. I said. I did. For the first year or two, mind your p's
and q's. Just zip it. Watch. Clock what's going on. You know
who likes jokes, I said. You know who likes that much chat.

Birds. He is. He's like a schoolgirl. An old washerwoman. Kids today. They've got no barriers. You can't teach 'em nothing. All triple-cocky. Got verbals to burn. I don't mind. I'll soak it up. But they've had a gut-full. They've had seconds. And thirds. So when I told them you'd rung, said Len's rung, they've said to me, they've said, 'Why don't you go and see him? See how he is. (*Beat*.) And when you go and see him, when you go down and see Len, why don't you take that little needler? Why don't you take that mouthy little bird.' He is. He's like a bird. A bird what you can't even shag. Although sometimes, you know. Just to shut him up. And at least now I won't have to listen to him moaning all the way home. 'My coffee's cold. My muffin's gone stale.'

Silence.

WEST. But –

WALLY. I can't make you, Len. I can't twist your arm. It's your decision. You want a lift? Back to London… Back home.

Silence.

WEST. GO AND WAIT IN THE CAR.

WALLY. You sure, Len? You don't have to…

Pause.

WEST. Go and wait in the car.

WALLY. That's the spirit. That's my Len. I'll tell you what? I'll be in the car, sunshine. And don't mention it, you prat. They'll be pleased as punch to see you. They'll be tickled pink. And you'll thank me for it. You'll see. You will, Len. You'll thank me for it.

He takes out a shiny black industrial bin liner.

Pop his head in here. They want to see it. (*Beat*.) I'll be in the car, Len. Ten minutes. Ten, then I'm off. If you want a lift… I'll be in the car. Ten minutes.

He turns. Then he turns back.

By the way, Len. This is… Look. About what happened… I just wanted to say… well. What I'm trying to say is…

(*Beat.*) Don't doze off. (*Beat.*) I know. I know. I'm just saying. This time. I know you won't. I know you'll do me
proud. But don't. Eh? I know you won't. But don't. Don't…
you know… Doze off. Don't make me come back up here.
You've got ten minutes. (*Beat.*)

Exit WALLY. WEST *is alone.*

PATSY (*off, upstairs. He comes downstairs*). Where's Wally?
He's not in his room. (*Pause.*)

WEST. You fix it, Patsy? You fix the suitcase?

PATSY. Where's Wally?

WEST. He's in the car.

PATSY. I see.

WEST. He's running the motor.

PATSY. Is he?

WEST. The ground froze. He's got it out. It's right as rain.

PATSY. That's good. (*Pause.*) So is he going back then? To
London.

WEST. London. Yes.

PATSY. I see. Well. I better get down there then. You not coming
along, Mr West?

WEST. See, that's the trouble, Patsy. It's a two-seater.

PATSY. Of course.

WEST. There's no room, see. There's only room for two.

PATSY. Of course there's not. Of course there is. I should have
thought of that.

WEST. You should have, Patsy. You should have.

Pause.

PATSY. Well I better be off. Don't want to keep Mr Coker
waiting.

PATSY *is shaking.*

He come in this morning. In the room. In the dark. He tells me. Why. Why he brung me. (*Beat.*) I'm their boy. They'll look after me. I'm in. I've just got to do one thing.

PATSY *takes out a black industrial bin liner.*

Silence. They stand opposite one another.

Enter LUE. *Pause.*

LUE. Look. He fixed it. He fixed my suitcase.

Silence.

What's going on? Len? What's happening?

Pause.

WEST. Well it's a very kind offer, Patsy. But as it turns out, I can't go to London today.

LUE. What? Where you going? What's going on?

WEST. That's just it. Even if there was enough room. Don't get me wrong. I'd love to, Patsy. Really I would. See, it's the pup. The pup's gone off. She's only small. (*Beat.*) So I can't up and leave her. She'd get back here, and I'd be gone. It's not fair.

PATSY. I suppose not.

WEST. The truth is, I can't, Patsy. I can't do it. (*Pause.*) Patsy is going to show you to the bus.

LUE. What do you mean? (*Pause.*)

WEST. Who knows, maybe he'll go with you to the airport. Maybe he'll go with you. See you get there safe. He could do with the sun on his face.

Beat. PATSY *nods.*

PATSY. Maybe I could. Yes. Maybe I could.

LUE. But… but… I'm not ready to go. I've not got my maps. And I've not got an alarm clock. And I need a spare costume, and a towel and –

WEST. Just go. Just go. Now.

LUE. But –

WEST. Go out the back door. Across the field. Go across the moor.

LUE. I can't. I need –

WEST. Go. Go now. You have to go. Now.

LUE. What are you going to do?

WEST. Just. Go.

LUE. I don't have the money –

PATSY. It's all right. I'll take you there. I've… I've got it. I've got money. Let's go.

LUE *looks from one to the other. She walks up to* WEST. *She kisses his cheek.*

LUE (*to* WEST). Take care of her. (*Pause.*)

They stand there, looking at each other. She turns and leaves. PATSY *follows.*

Silence. A plane approaches. It tears over. Then fades.

WEST *is alone.*

He goes to the kitchen. He takes out the dog food. He comes back out.

WEST. Dolly. Dolly, Din Dins. Din Dins, Dolly. Dolly. Din Dins.

WEST *picks up the axe and sits, the axe across his lap.*

He waits.

Dolly. Din Dins. Din Dins. Dolly. Din Dins.

He sits there.

Fade to black.

The End.